Three Reflections, One World

By

Kura Amatulla

ISBN: 1-4033-1644-9 (Softcover)
ISBN: 1-4033-1643-0 (Electronic)

This book is printed on acid free paper.

1stBooks - rev. 04/04/02

Table of Contents

Introduction .... *vii*

On Love: Inhale.............................. *1*

Aroma *3*
Describe Me.................................. *5*
The Picture Before the Reality and Still She Has Fear.... *9*
War Won Over the Fear *11*
Special Occasions............................ *13*
Beauty Personified........................... *15*
Green *17*
A Good Kind of Spoiled....................... *19*
Creamy...................................... *23*

Issues In between: Why I Went There...........25

Three Reflections, One World..................27

A Seed Was Planted............................29

Getting Dirty...................................33

Oh My God...What Have I Done?..............35

No Doubt...Right???............................37

The Look.......................................39

Mum's The Word, Until You've Had Enough........41

Finding Joy on A Rainy Day..................43

I Wanna Laugh... 45

Dolls Have No Souls 47

Grateful.......................................49

Have You Seen My Friend? 51

Engraved Invitations.........................53

I'd Rather Be Alone...........................55

Don't Change Your Way.......................57

I Wonder 59

Untitled.......................................61

On Pain: Time to Release *63*

A Reflection of Prior Innocence.................. *65*
Too Far to The Left, When it Should Have Been Right... *67*
The Last Time it Happened.................... *69*
Ever Been Screwed? *71*
How Do You Spell Release? *73*
The Conscious Rape.......................... *75*
The Laws of His Nature....................... *77*
Sophisticated Slavery......................... *79*
That's Not It *81*
Wasted Opportunity *83*
Like Cuss Words to Me........................ *85*
For The One Who Will Come After Me............ *87*
You missed the Soul of me *89*

Introduction

Hello Reader,

This is my very first expose in the world of poetry. For many years I have spoken to many who know me regarding the prospect of my publishing a book. These very people I refer to used to read my notebooks and give me such praise. They made me feel as though they understood where I was coming from, and in giving them comfort-it gave me comfort. With that comfort, I became strengthened. It is with that strength and love for writing that I share this with you. I hope that you will reflect and be comforted as well. Enjoy.

On Love: Inhale

I think we can all recall the newness with which each relationship was begun.

We remember the tumble of our stomachs or how we would close our eyes as that special someone passed by…just to smell their breeze as they went by.

This portion of poems will be dealing with some of the innocence that comes with new relationships. Inhale and enjoy.

Aroma

Hm, you smell that?
That's the smell of Right Now;
with a hint of Back Then
It's mixed with the sweetness of
Remember When

It's the smell of Today;
with a fogginess of Tomorrow
The smell of Past, Present, and Future
you know

Hm, Today is
Right Now it's
Hm, Yesterday was

It's smelling pretty good

Describe Me

Better in scent, sense, or sight?
All pretty sweet
Pecan-tan in cold, Dark, Dark Bronze in heat
38-36-Forty I don't know
Huggable anyway
Average height
A woman and a lady
Even kissable…maybe
With a voice notable for it's "900-Number" quality
A Heart that may have love for you
All that and Brains too!

Are You Sweet on Me???

You sat quietly
Gave an occasional smile; a wave to say "hi"
You didn't intrude on my daily affairs; just let my go by
One day you inquired
And shyly stood
I didn't keep going as I normally would

We reflected in quiet; sometimes after dark
Sat side by side, looked in each others eyes, and sometimes we talked

You gave of your time
If I asked, you would do
I had to wonder, "Is he sweet on me?" and decide what to do

A time came when we had to go back to our own sides
To tie up loose ends, achieve closures; figure what (for us) in the future lies

I came to understand that I had been wrong to conclude
That I didn't know what or what to feel about someone so real as you

Good thing I didn't close that door
Our future is scripting so much more

I'm asking you now
What I should've then
When I thought you'd only be an associate, a friend

For all that you have done
And what you stand to do

Are you sweet on me?
Because I'm sweet on you

The Picture Before the Reality and Still She Has Fear

The courtship of sorts begins

He's not touched her yet; but he's gotten her attention

Says he doesn't want a long term thing

Cause circumstances couldn't bear it now...

It'd be depressing

He makes love to her mind; saying that he'd never hurt her

He stills the evenings with blissful words; conferring with her

Conversation, like orgasm, is momentary

After the pleasure there comes reality

The picture appears beautiful but there's been no room made on the wall

She's been here before

And it wasn't as it appeared at all

So she goes home alone and cries for strength through loneliness...

Tear after tear

She sees the picture before the reality and still she has fear

War Won Over the Fear

Persistence is what finished it
As patience was constantly tried
Love stepped in, in a strong form
When fear let me think that I'd died

He's well within the limits.
His deen is tight
Brightness shows all over him
So it's not hard to see the light

God sent a bounteous blessing
When he set "War" on my path
To strike a blow to the things
I'd long felt caused me wrath

I tried so hard to stay alone
So no one could see my tears
As loneliness was staking its claim to me,
"War" won over the fear

Was it a sign I should've reflected on long ago?

I guess

Was it the charitable smile that welcomed me each time we've met?

Why yes

Wisdom tore at the fortress I'd built, brick by brick

Other inquisitive minds just felt he was a good pick

Recently, the days have been filled with much prayer; only joy has caused the tears

For loneliness will become unknown to me

Since "War" won over the fear

Special Occasions

Waking up and Giving Praise
To the One who let it be
Lathering up with your favorite scent
Simplicity, that's special to me

Putting on your favorite clothes
Down to that raggedy pair of shoes
Singing the Gospel of Gratitude
Leaving off the blues

That first cup of coffee
Put together just right
A hard scrambled omelet with veggies and cheese,
Just plain out of sight

Smooth commute
Towards the deeds of the day
Numerous blessings
As you make your way.

These are the days to live for…

Beauty Personified

Average height and average build
A bit above average in places I was allowed to go
You know

A "Special Dark" candy bar skin tone
With lips so hot pink, so soft
Beautiful hands he had...brains
We had a Love Jones
So strong

He worked the same as Jordan dunked
...with his tongue out
I used to love to watch his differences and my likeness make contact
With those eyes, that grin, those hands...

My God, thank you for allowing me to hold him
Forever in me
For he was...Beauty personified

Green

More than just a color
Or the name of a brother
Green is a unique hue
It is the shade of money
Or a four leaf clover
Green is new
It is you
It can take on an ugly form
If envy replaces charm
Yes, Green is a unique hue
Enjoy its form
For Green is a norm
Otherwise, it will turn blue

A Good Kind of Spoiled

He wants to feed me
With food cooked by his hand

He wants to still the time with warmth and
Conversation
Show me the true meaning of gentleman

We've not touched physically,
But he's claiming a part of my heart

A simple woman on a beautiful day capturing a special thought

Already Under My Skin

I close my eyes and begin to smile
I'm thinking and this may go on for a while
I remember
your eyes
your touch
your smile
and from within I quiver because
You're already under my skin
My eyes are still closed and nobody knows
I'm feeling…feeling you
from head to toe
Your shell to my shell
mild friction causing both bodies to swell
I'm feeling your heart
It's rhythm-filled beating, throbbing from inside my private parts
We sing soft love songs to one another
to others It sounds like passion-filled
prayers, lamitations, moans…
Your lips all over
Your hands in mine

Your movement so awesome
so pure
divine
Flashes of what could be
what should be…what is
But no regrets from either one of doing this…
My eyes are still closed
and nobody knows
I'm feeling…have felt you
from head to toe
I open my eyes and I still smile
this reflection has gone on for quite a while
I hug myself as I recall
your eyes, the look
your touch, the hands
your smile, the lips
and from within
I quiver because you're still under my skin

Creamy

You

You got me

Hot

Bothered

Warm

Tingly

Smiling

Dreaming

Hungry

Ready

Waiting

Tight

Baby,

You got me creamy

Issues In between: Why I Went There

Three Reflections, One World

Three women stood in awe of the world
One was Creamy Light
One was Pecan Tanned
The last was Special Dark, with curls

Pecan wondered how she would survive
Special knew it'd be a struggle
Creamy didn't give it a second Thought, for she knew how she'd thrive

Special wondered when or if her struggle would end
Creamy didn't know of such a thing; for while everyone she knew was toiling and struggling, she would reap whatever her smile would bring
Creamy looked over the world
And figured it would be an easy task
Pecan thought of all the unanswered questions about Man that she wanted to ask

Special looked up, then down, and then just stared at the two other women
She said that Creamy would be all right

But Pecan, well she'd become a powerful Muslim

Pecan was shocked into reflection right then

She had to chuckle to herself about getting the run-down leftovers of Creamy's and Special's men

But then she held her head up high and patted herself on the back

The thought of Islam taking over her life would free her from this pack

Creamy wanted what none of them had

She left for the world and life got pretty bad

She turned to a life of stealing and cheating and men who kept her crying

Or due for more beating

Special wondered into a world all her own

Though very educated and strong, she ended up miserable and alone

Year's later, Pecan thought about Creamy's state of being

And Special's kind words

And what was said and done during the time

When the women stood in awe of the world

A Seed Was Planted

A seed was planted a long time ago
When dropped, the seed was nowhere near soil
No one was there to tend and care
So the seed remained closed and rolled on

One year, the seed rolled into some sand
No way was the sand fertile for a seed to plant
The first some ever seen
Cause the seed to sprout…it became a weed
Melancholy, bitter, and neglected…the weed recoiled back into a seed
Safe haven for the rejected

Wind caused the seed to wander into soil
The seed was almost comfortable; the soil was moist
Being mysterious and misleading, the soil opened a pocket for the seed to fall into
It wasn't known that other seeds were in the midst and that this seed shouldn't have fallen there…
But the soil didn't care
The soil grew cold and then turned warm
Guess it was the lull before the storm

The seed reopened into a blossom
The blossom thought it was Spring
But then the soil grew too cold…not again!

The soil spit it out and its roots began to recoil
It wanted to die after this second time
After rejection from the soil
But the rays wouldn't let it give up

The blossom recoiled back into a seed
The life in it drained, so it was free of need
The sell became hard to protect against the elements
It wandered under a rock, a sort of defense

Closed, protected, and still neglected…
The seed was cautious, but waiting for the nurturing soil it would need
To make a place to safe guard the seed

The seed was called to nurturing soil
No more rolling back into a coil
No more mystery and coldness…for Spring is here
Maybe the hand that handles this seed will take care…

Real care that's sorely needed
No stomping, no sand, no neglect
Or being misleaded

Finally, there will be no more cold
Maybe this seed will finally get to become
A Rose

Getting Dirty

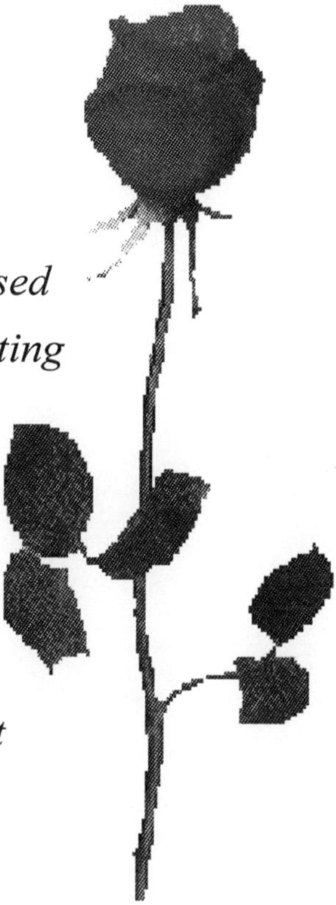

Girls…listen to one who knows
One who's fell down
Got dirty
One that'll tell you how it goes
Don't wait until you get tired of being used
Being groped and tasted and then getting screwed
Pay attention to all the signs
The late nights out
The screaming and shouting
Those "kiss-n-makeup" pacifier lines
Remain as you were before you met
Keep your smile
Your strength
Keep your goals set
Where ever you go and decide to do
Allow no one to hurt…
No on to lie…
Allow no one to throw their dirt on you

Oh My God…What Have I Done?

In Your Name, It was begun as something new
Quite immediately, I adjusted to three, from two
But a change hasn't come yet on his side
For I am not treated as some blushing bride

At times, I feel this effort is so strong
But my caring, support, my strength seem to make me wrong
Surely, I hope all these efforts are for you
But as it gets to be too much in other things, it means he doesn't need us two

It would mean he wants the extras and he doesn't mean to share
For technically we are in Contract…he may not even care
Apparently, I don't give him the satisfaction that that does
So I wonder where the love went that once was

Did I get into a relationship that he'd already established with life?

Because for as much as he's gone and how he leaves, he didn't want a wife

Oh Lord, really I don't want to complain about this you see

Because originally I was fighting to stay lonely

I explained why I shouldn't get married and the priceless things I'd need

But he just goes on…he doesn't take heed

I'm already feeling pangs of regret

Mainly because I'm dealing with neglect

For money, his other spouse, keeps him hemmed up

And his life-plans were for his people first; so we don't fit the tea in that cup

I knew that marriage isn't meant to be all fun

But I wonder what I should do now about what I have done

If I'm silent, I'm wrong

If I laugh, I've talked too long

Was I wrong to accept a husband for Your will to be fulfilled?

Because though I can paste on many smiles, I feel my spirit's been killed

No Doubt…Right???

I gave in
I'm trying again
To be a good woman; fit for a good man
He's let me see
Some pleasure, some peace
And he's taught life changing lessons to me
So why is a question mark creeping in?
Why am I wondering if I should've waited again?
He says he loves me…
I say the same every night
So there should be no doubt in this decision…
Right???

The Look

He gives me the look when the deeds are done
He gives me that look and knows that I'm stunned
He gives me the look when he comes back around
And when he does, slightly I frown

I try to go on and paste on a smile
But this keeps on
happening all
the while

That look
means many
things to me
No one else will get that look you see
What they'll get is the greatest side
That smile that's big, beautiful, and wide

They'll never see or feel the pangs I took
To hold myself together
Each time he gave me the look

Mum's The Word, Until You've Had Enough

Make no comments!
Men don't like that sort of thing
For even if you are a good woman
It can ruin your mental well-being

Use paper and prayer to release!
It doesn't rehash old, dead news
You have the convenience of writing both views
It doesn't dominate or point down at you
When finished, you tend to feel better too

Men, like customers, are supposed to be right…even when they are not
Bite your tongue!

When your nerves are all uptight
And you've begun to lose your appetite
Because you know he's not going to be right
Before you lose sight
Pack…
Your time to take flight might be that night

Or stay in a Mum's World

Finding Joy on A Rainy Day

My favorite cloth has the smell of

Mountain Springs

My pillows are soft and fluffy

My eyes and limbs work pretty well

My child is fairly healthy

I get to hear my daughter's call and watch her grow beautifully

Tall

I live

I eat, sleep, and breathe

I am grateful

Even once the rain has stopped

I Wanna Laugh…

…As if there were no bills to pay
…As though there were no clouds today
…Like a child in a park
…And be as happy as a lark
I've spent too much time being blue
And blaming myself for what you say and do
I'm getting on up and dusting off the dirt,
and dropping off the baggage labeled "pain & hurt"
I wanna laugh
…As if I've won the lottery
…Because I'm fine being me
…And know that all is well
…While I bury this hardened shell
I wanna laugh
…As if there were no clouds today or
…Even if it's raining all day
I'm gonna laugh and smile…all day today

Dolls Have No Souls

Sometimes I'd wish it was painted on
A smile
That way, I wouldn't have to feel
Fake
All the while

I'd wish that I didn't have to be fed
Not have to care for myself
Occasionally bring joy to a child or
Be content to collect dust upon a shelf
Wouldn't care
Wouldn't dream
Wouldn't know how to laugh
No need or reason to scream
Just be…a Doll

Now as I breathe
I care
I dream
I love to laugh
Try to avoid screaming

I am human, a woman
And grateful for the good and bad to behold
I could never be…a Doll
Because they have no souls

Grateful

It is my name
And due to too much kindness,
Sometimes my shame
Because of a lot of giving,
My lack of fortune and fame

But I keep being me and I am
Grateful

Have You Seen My Friend?

O God, I seem to have lost my friend
He promised he'd be there
Until the end
He said he loved me and that he cared
But he's gone now and I know not where

How will I go on? What can I do?
Things were so good between us two
He used to smile; we hugged so much
Now I'm missing the warmth of his touch

His eyes were so gentle
His smile almost glowed
He knew me in ways
No one will know
Is he lost to the world that's beyond our control?
Lord, please send me a vision that I might be consoled

Have you seen my friend?
He's lost you see
Look for him…Pray for him
Bring him back to me

Engraved Invitations

I *am fresh from the shower, as I'm prone to be*

I try to keep myself clean you see

He grins as I turn away; I know what that's going to mean for me

He poses in the mirror and likes what e sees

I sigh, shake my head, and keep my focus on the T.V.

He pulls on his bottoms and the shirt he's going to wear

I look down at bare breasts and thong underwear

Earlier in the day and many before

I'm treated like tissue, a mat, and then a swinging door

He's coming my way

Oh no, he's coming my way

Going to grope and touch and not say much

He's going to make a run…

I wonder why I've not sent out invitations

I'd Rather Be Alone

I could be held and holding
Someone and me
I could dismiss my cares and think of only
Someone and me
I could complain of not having enough time for
Someone and me

But I'd rather be alone, and keep the peace

Peace can be sort of a lonely thing
It causes struggle…reflection
Evasiveness and rejection
Peace can cause heartbreak and tears

Because…

I can't be held and holding
Someone and me
I can't dismiss my fears and think of only
Someone and me

I'm too scared to allow time for
Someone and me

For I'd care too much; so I'd rather be alone
And keep the peace

Don't Change Your Way

When asking God for something good
We should all reflect
When or if this blessing comes,
Would we always give our best?

Would we shine it up, polish it, and give it tender care?
Or would we change and treat that blessing...
As if a burden to bear

Would we act like someone else and treat the blessing awfully bad?
Or would we talk to and treat it like the best thing we ever had?

Never make yourself out to be more than human; that would make you a lie
And God can take it all from you with no apparent reason why
Then you'd want to hurt the blessing and cause it undo pain
And to hide the mess you've made...ask for blessings again

Your blessing(s) stand in front of God
Evidence then places blame
You then reflect on what you did
And bring light to your shame

You see dear brother, when you were blessed,
You somehow lost faith
Then as time went on, you showed your blessing(s) unkindness, coldness, hate

God heard the cries of your blessing(s); then he took it from you
Consider the mercy with what's left over
Because He could've taken your life
Too

I Wonder

You
Love me?
You
Care?
And yet you're always gone...
There?
You
Want me?
Oh really?
And yet you have me questioning my abilities
Ok
What's next?
Another minute of
Unwanted sex?
You love me?
Sure you do
Even more when I'm
Away from you

Untitled…

Once, you've denied yourself a potential blessing
Two or more times; with no thought of a reason why
After a time, and some reflection, it comes around again
Will you accept or deny?

Sunshine is glorious, but not in a boastful way
It shines on you, nurtures you, is there for you all day

But if you stay shut in and block yourself from the beauty that is the sun
You can't complain if it's dark and the moon is in place of what's gone

Another opportunity to take in the rays of sweet sunny radiance
It's come for you again today
But if you continue to deny yourself its benefits
The sunshine doesn't stay

On Pain: Time to Release

A Reflection of Prior Innocence

He said we were going to play a game
He was around 19, I think "J" was his name
Since that day, life has been forever changed
For I was innocent no more…

How was I to know this game or its rules
Looking back on what he did; it was cruel
He said if I cry, I was going to get it
I was but a child of four…

Mama went shopping with a girlfriend you see
So she wasn't there when he took what was prized; me
I remained a good girl and kept my mouth shut
Though, down there, I was really sore…

I'm a woman now and I know what it is
For a man to touch something, take something that's knowingly not his
Some call it stealing, rape, or molestation
I thought it made me ugly, poor…

I told mama in my own little way
Big people weren't talked down about; by kids in that day
Maybe she would've thought I was a fast little girl
But I was simply innocent...no more...

I'm a mother now with a better outlook
I've moved forward, regardless of what he took
Since that day, life has been changed
And today, I reflect on Prior Innocence.

Too Far to The Left, When it Should Have Been Right

The piece won't fit anymore
It's just there
Shoved, cramped, and crooked
Just laying any old way

Even if I turn it
It's no use
The ends are all stripped and worn
from years of abuse

If I said, "Baby, please…today?"
He'd reply with "Tomorrow night"

Could change at the drop of a dime
And I worry all the time
I keep changing my mind
And staying on…while trying not to whine

That opening is done for now
Space is getting tight

This heart's been slapped
Too far to the left
When it should have been
Stroked to the right

The Last Time it Happened

The last time it happened, he said it wouldn't happen again
He said that his intention was never to inflict pain
He knew that she'd been there before
He knew that she'd cried
But then he did it once again...a part of her just died

The last time it happened, he said it didn't make him feel good
To not be able to communicate
in the way he should
He told her that he loved her
He said their thing was strong
Well now, it's happened again...something went terribly wrong

The last time it happened
Was after she professed to public ear
That...loneliness would become unknown to me now that
"War Won Over the Fear"
Fear has not returned just yet, for she has become quite cold

She's wondering whether or not to believe
Anything she was ever told
The events that took place have really torn them apart
That look, that touch, that voice she hears
Has really broken her heart

The last time it happened
He said it wouldn't happen again
Somehow she thought that apology was supposed to make a mend
He knew that she'd been there before
He knew that she'd cried
But then he did it once again
A part of her just died

He told her that he loved her
He said their thing was strong
But seeing that it's happened again
She'll do better to be alone

Ever Been Screwed?

Let me tell you how it feels
Just a human's point of view
So you'll know what to look for
Incase someone tries you

It smiles,
It's gentle and oh so smooth
It will patiently wait
For the chance to get you

It sets the trap
And you're as good as doomed
For now you must prepare to be
Royally screwed

That alluring smile fades
And frowns take it's place
Whatever nice things that came from those lips
Slow in pace

That gentle person has now turned hardcore
For once it gets you
Love resides there no more

Just wanted to give forewarning
Just a human's point of view
So you know what to look for
And won't get yourself screwed

How Do You Spell Release?

C - ***__Continue__*** *to let him in whether he loves you or not*

U - ***__Undress__*** *as quickly as possible. He won't have a lot of time*

M - ***__Make__*** *his "Woo". Swerve as if it's your last experience or at least get him off*

S - ***__Say__*** *very little. If you are not stroking his ego, he has not need of conversation*

A - ***__Allow__*** *him to speak and do to you as he wishes; that's supposed to be helping him*

C - ***__Continue__*** *until he drops his…if you get yours then good for you*

K - ***__Keep__*** *a lid on it! You keep your mouth closed; he comes back for more*

The Conscious Rape

No!

No!

Why won't you hear me?

Can't you see?

If you do it, it will continue to eat at me!

No!

Stop it!

Please don't do this!

It won't make you more than a monster

Damn, and you want a kiss?

Why?

Why continue?

So what if I just bathed

Oh

Now you love me…

And think that's the key to my gate

So you just gonna take it?

All puffed up with pride
Leaving that crap in me
As evidence of your ride

No!
No!
This does not feel good!
No, you are not a man!
No, you don't love me!
I am not pretty right now
You've made me dirty, ugly!
I'm shamed and I didn't want this
It's worse than screwing
It's conscious rape

The Laws of His Nature

Woke up this morning
And learned something new
His nature isn't what's the same
For me and you

The sky can be bright
Or a brilliant shade or hue
He'll call it something else
And refuse to hear the truth

The winds can be light
Giving joy of a cool breeze
He'll wear a coat
As though he would freeze

Time was once a normal concept
Known to any other man
But a minute to him typically means
If or when he can

When dealing with him you must understand
Normal concepts don't apply
He'll conveniently manipulate, guilt you,
Or lie

Laid down tonight
And thought to myself
Maybe I should keep this knowledge
On the shelf
His nature isn't what's the same
For me and you
But naw, he can continue to hide…
Because I know the truth

Sophisticated Slavery

Us git fed as you see fit
We's git clothes after you git
Not goin up side my head no mo
Massa be flexin while the servants is po
Us be livin as ya thank we should
You's be thankin this is livin good
You's be gone mos days and nights
Can't ask questions
That's another fight
Supposed to be a partnership betwixt you and me
But you's just the massa of my
Slavery

That's Not It

Does it lie within the idle promises;
Made just to pacify?
Or in the mouth that is frowned
Just before it begins to cry?
Maybe it's in the sex
That's now taken...cus' I'm clean
I'm not allowed to call it "rape";
though true, it just sounds mean
Could it be in the many nights;
And days I spend alone?
No, that can't be it
Because there's no love being shown.

Wasted Opportunity

I awoke early

Again today

To see a certain beauty that only shows itself

When you are asleep

But

You weren't there, not here, not anywhere near

I went about the day as though I was blazing with your charm, your love, your heart

But then my heart faded back to dark

When I came home, your body was here, but you still were not

My head aches

Your mouth banged at the door:

You want your hair done today

Oh, but you'll pay me another day

You called about my head being done

Yeah, uh huh

You just want you taken care of

Then you'll be gone again

Yet, for a moment, I think we saw something
I think we both felt something
Or at least I did
The opportunity to say "I'm sorry" went away

Like Cuss Words to Me

Love *has bitten*

I'm more than twice shy

Got ***promises*** *to avoid*

I don't ask

What

When

Or why

For now, ***marriage*** *is a No-No*

Just go on and go so

These terms will no longer be

Like cuss words to me

For The One Who Will Come After Me

He's going to smile and melt your heart
He's going to spend time; run some lines
But you should be warned from the start

He likes his women a particular way
If you're smiling now
Later you'll remember; if you decide you can't stay

I can't say he'll do the same as what he did to me
I just want to send a warning
For the one who will come after me

Time may become a concept that is unknown
You might sit and wait; and agonize all alone
Give it up girl because he won't be coming home

Be ready to be scrutinized with whatever you've done or said
He's gonna say and do some things in the present
But he's gonna hold your past over your head

He like him some sex girl

That's good if you like yours

But keep an eye open for when he takes it as though you're his free little whore

He going to smile and melt your heart

He's going to spend time, run some lines

But I just want to warn you from the start

No, I can't say that he'll do the same

As what he did to me

I'm just being a woman and sending a warning

For the one who'll come after me

You missed the Soul of me

I sit and marvel…sometimes

I know that if it were not for God's Grace and Mercy, I would not be

The sweet disposition standing before you

The one who used to believe your every word and in your every dream

But you got me

Good

I offered all of me…

Because of love

You took, and handed very little back

Took some more-some I didn't know I had

Along with almost all my dignity

It hurt

To see such beauty become so monstrous

Such softness become so hard

Such warmth turn so cold

But boldly

You are so perfectly justified…or so you feel

I sit and marvel…I even giggle sometimes

I know I came with no warranty

I've gone a long time with no care
Got a lot of wear and tear
But I thank God, for I am Blessed to Be,
And for all that you got
You missed the Soul of me

About the Author

Kura Amatulla originates from St. Louis, Missouri.

Since childhood, she has always had an appreciation for the therapy within creative forms of expression.

Throughout her teen and early adult years, she learned to reflect and release her thoughts, trials, and journeys into various journals that she keeps to this day.

Venturing toward the land of "thirty and above", she is now pursuing her life-long love of writing and sharing her works with the world.

www.ingramcontent.com/pod-product-compliance
Ingram Content Group UK Ltd.
Pitfield, Milton Keynes, MK11 3LW, UK
UKHW041933190726
13854UKWH00004B/1564